AF489277

contents

Elements

Love, Earth, Fire, Wind, and Water.
The natural chaos of creativity is exciting and adverse.
To love of Earth's creations is to love her.
The wild and mild natures, the Universe.

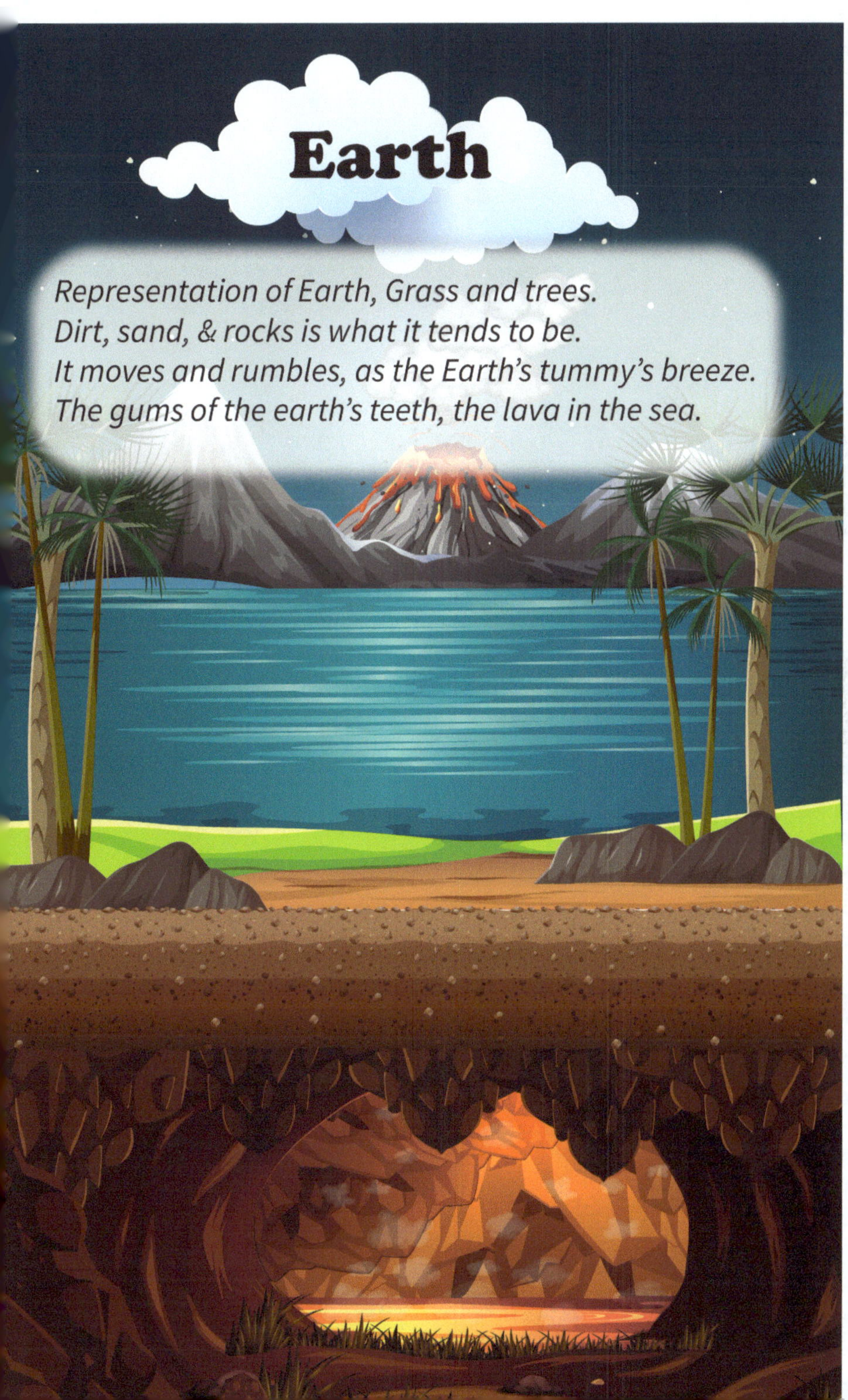

Earth

Representation of Earth, Grass and trees.
Dirt, sand, & rocks is what it tends to be.
It moves and rumbles, as the Earth's tummy's breeze.
The gums of the earth's teeth, the lava in the sea.

Air

The breath of the earth as it needs to breathe.
The blow of air, oh so wild.
Wind is above ground but, not underneath.
The love I have for air is calm and mild.

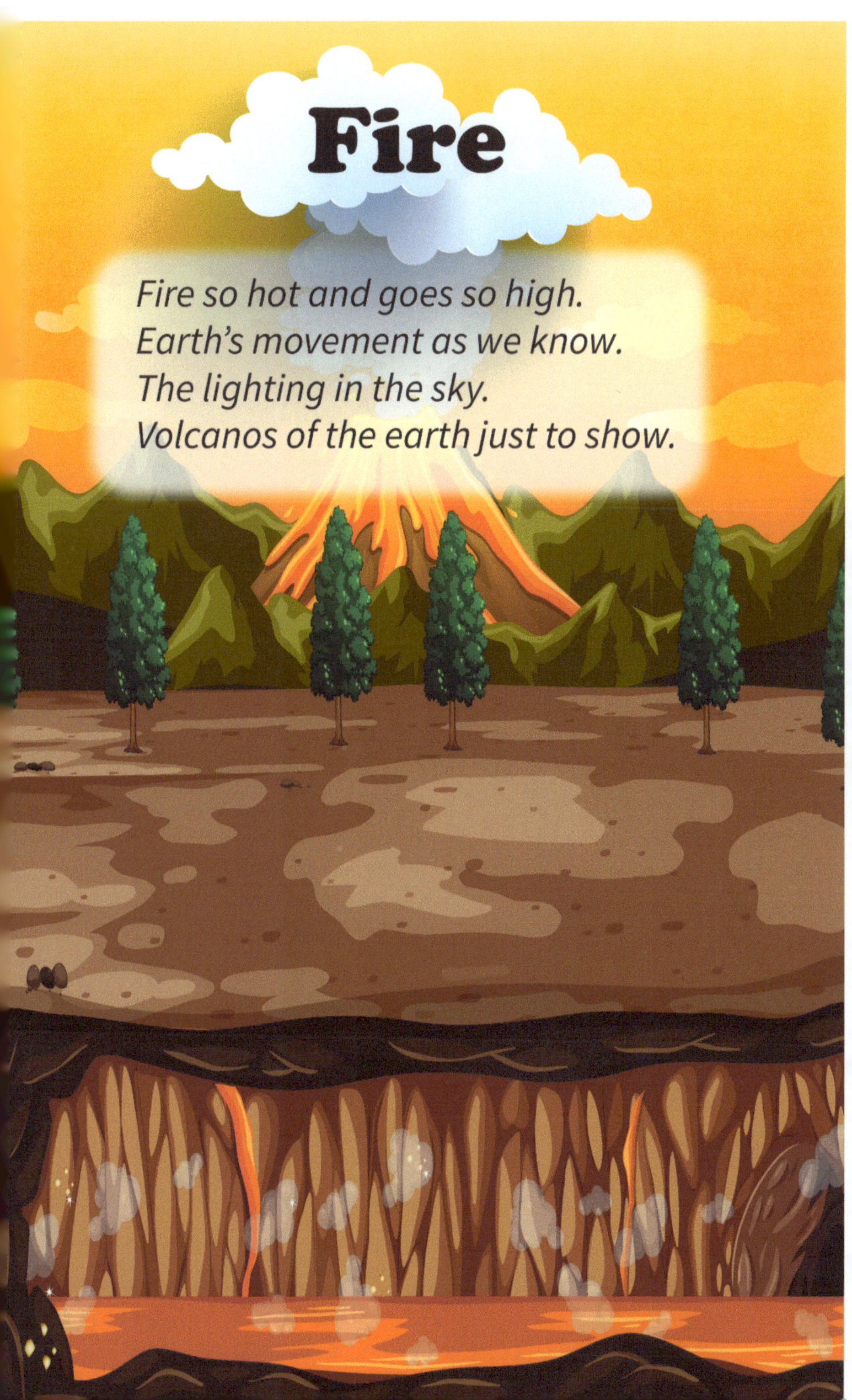

Fire

Fire so hot and goes so high.
Earth's movement as we know.
The lighting in the sky.
Volcanos of the earth just to show.

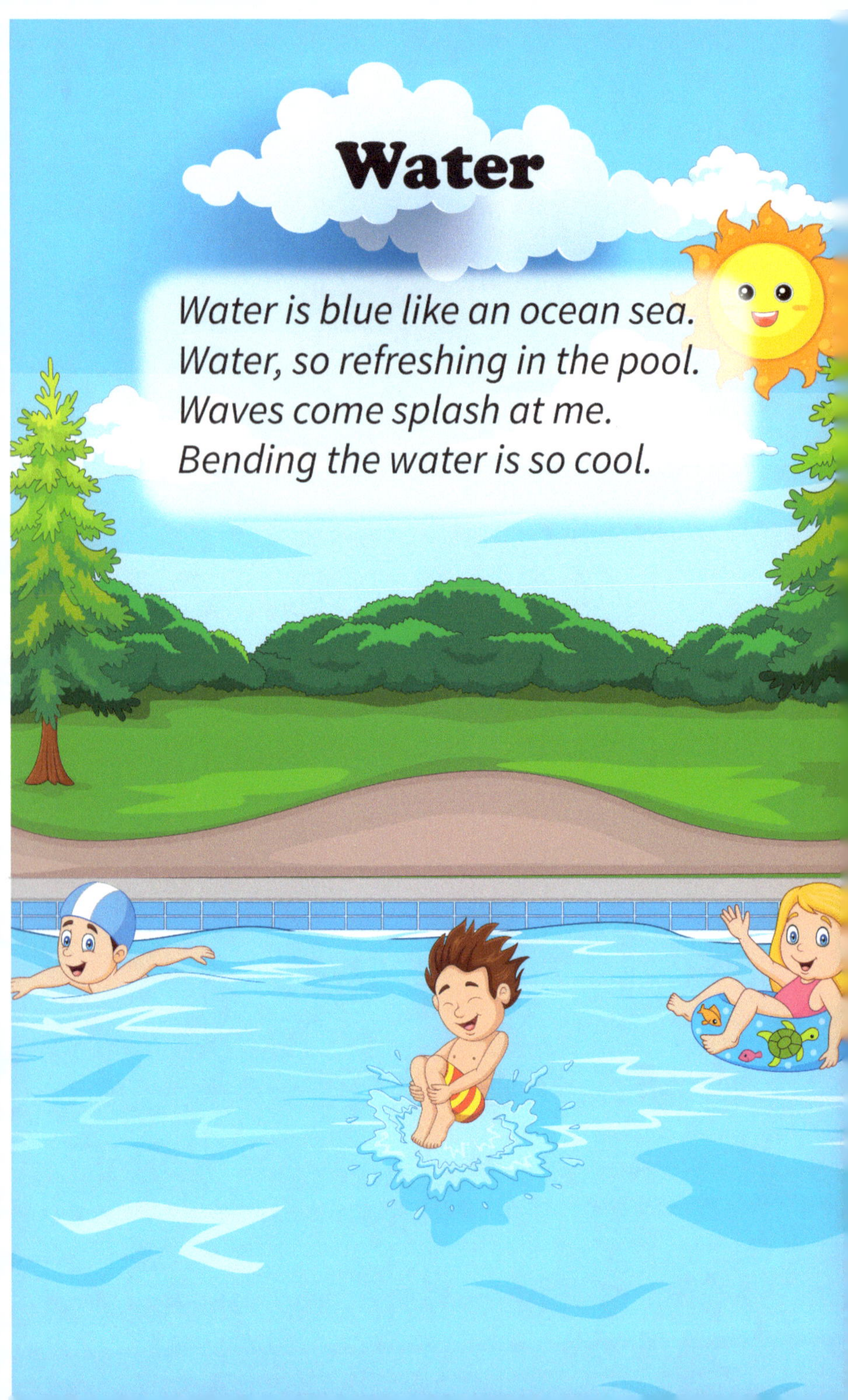

Water

Water is blue like an ocean sea.
Water, so refreshing in the pool.
Waves come splash at me.
Bending the water is so cool.

Love

The only element that you can not see.
Eternity life cycle of unconditional emotions.
With out it, there would not be life before me.
Family, father, mother, daughters, sons.

Food and Drink

Carrots dance like a worm in the sand.
Water will splash if drinks do that dance.
So, carrots keep dancing in the plate until they can't anymore.
I ate the carrots.
The drink gets the last dance as it goes down my throat.

Words mean everything

Words mean everything.
Nice words, mean words, all words mean something.
We can test words like a spelling bee.
Words mean everything to me.

Do you see that shark?
Umm... guys do you see that shark over there?
Are you scared of sharks?
What are you guys doing?
Well, they kill about 10 people per year.

Do you want food?

Hi sir, do you want food?
Yeah, I will order a burger.
Sorry, we are out of burgers
Would you like something else?
No, but I would like a smoothie.

Money

Money doesn't grow on trees.
Money is made from trees.
Not made from leaves.
But green like leaves.

Forest Stew

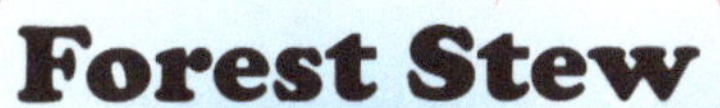

Trees, leaves, where are you?
I can't find my friends.
I am lost! Searching, Searching, still Searching…
2 hours later…
I wake up, It was a dream?

Solar Stew

Sun, stars are you here?
Nobody can see me.
At least I get to see our solar stew.
Learning space is great
So much to learn, so much we don't see.
And soon they will all know me as the greatest star to be.

Game Night

Games, family, what else could you ask for?
Monopoly, Battleship, Uno, Trouble, chutes and ladders, hungry hippo, & Sorry.
Spending time with family, I ask for more.
The best day of the week, to me.

Dreamland

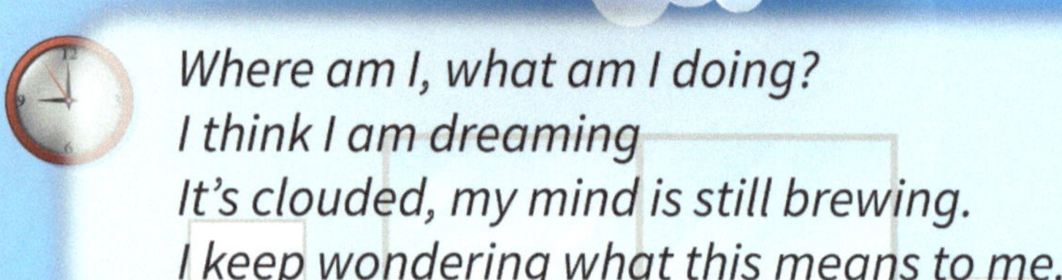

Where am I, what am I doing?
I think I am dreaming
It's clouded, my mind is still brewing.
I keep wondering what this means to me.

Colorful

Red, orange, blue, what color are you?
I see you green, purple, and black.
You too grey and white.
The rainbow has might.

You

You are like a star in my eyes.
Your brightness shows as life is so bright.
Yet, your eyes are like fireworks.
Bursting in the skies.

Pizza Party

Pizza party at my house.
Sausage, pepperoni, and bacon too.
No one can sleep through it, not even a mouse.
The only friends that don't come are the ones that say "achoo"!

Sugar Rush

Sugar, candy, cake.
I love it all.
Some takes time to bake.
When I have a lot, I have a ball.

Light
So light, so bright.
The biggest star is the sun.
I can't wait til it's night.
Off, on, as each day gets done.

Bright Future ahead of me

Mirror, mirror on the wall.
As I stand in front of you what do you see.
I stand here confident and tall.
What you set your mind to is what you will be.

Dreamland

Introducing "Dreamland: A Book of Poetry" by a Talented Nine-Year-Old Author.

Step into the enchanting world of "Dreamland," a captivating collection of poetry written by a remarkable nine-year-old author. With boundless imagination and a unique perspective, this young wordsmith takes readers on a mesmerizing journey through the realms of dreams, emotions, and wonder.

In this heartfelt compilation, each poem is a window into the author's vivid dreams and innermost thoughts. From whimsical tales of talking animals to poignant reflections on friendship and love, "Dreamland" invites readers of all ages to explore the limitless possibilities of the imagination.

With a lyrical and evocative writing style, the young author effortlessly weaves words together, painting vibrant pictures with each line. Through their innocent and authentic voice, they capture the essence of childhood innocence and the beauty of seeing the world through untainted eyes.

"Dreamland" is not just a book of poetry; it is a testament to the power of dreams and the limitless potential of young minds. It serves as an inspiration to aspiring young writers and a reminder to adults of the magic that lies within us all.

Experience the enchantment of "Dreamland" and be transported to a world where dreams come alive. Join the journey of this extraordinary nine-year-old author and discover the power of imagination through the art of poetry.